3

Theme

Sw.   Foundations 8, 4, 2; Mixtures; Sw. to Gt. 8
Gt.   Foundations 8, 4, 2; Mixtures
Ch.   Foundations 8, 4, 2; Mixtures; Ch. to Gt.
Ped. Foundations 16, 8; Sw. to Ped.

Stately

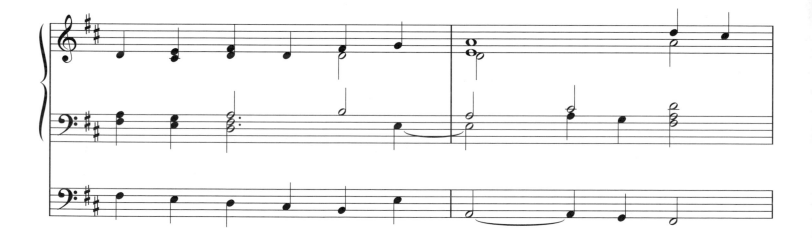

+Sw. Reed 4

+Sw. Reed 16

cresc. to end

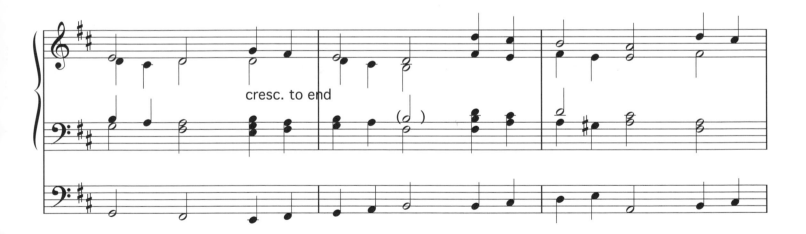

+Sw. to Gt. 4

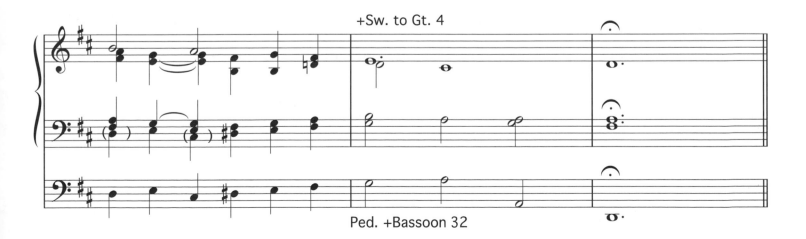

Ped. +Bassoon 32

Scherzo

Sw.   Strings; Sw. to Ch.
Gt.   ---------
Ch.   Strings
Ped.   Small Reed 4; trem.

9

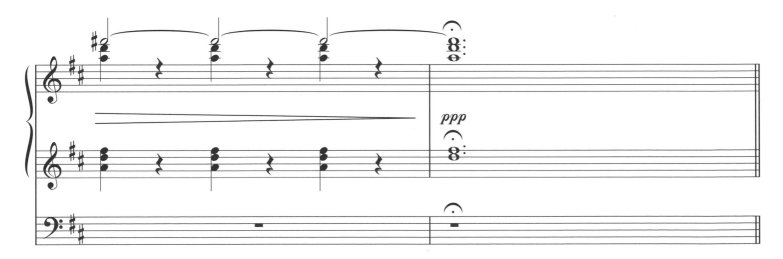

March

Sw.   Foundations 8, 4, 2; Mixtures; Tpt. 8
Gt.   Solo Tpt. (*ff*)
Ch.   Solo Tpt. (*f*)
Ped. Foundations 16, 8; Sw. to Ped.

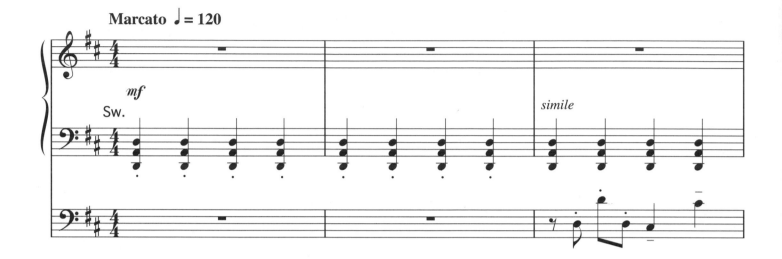

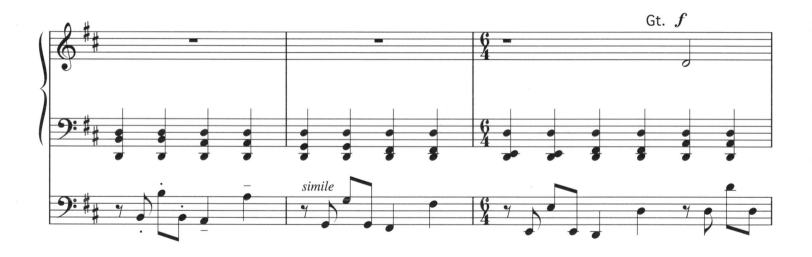

Adagio

Sw.   Strings
Gt.   Flute 8; Sw/Ch 8, 4 to Gt.
Ch.   Strings; Flute 8; Sw. to Ch.
Ped.   16, 8; Sw/Ch to Ped.

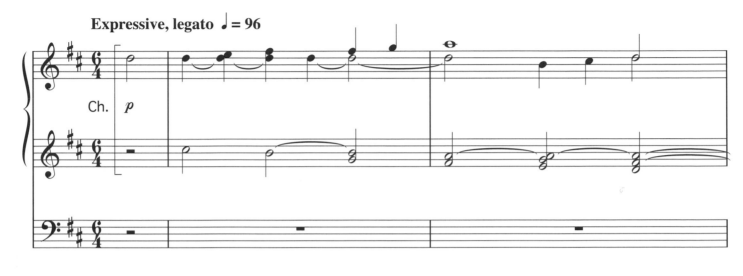

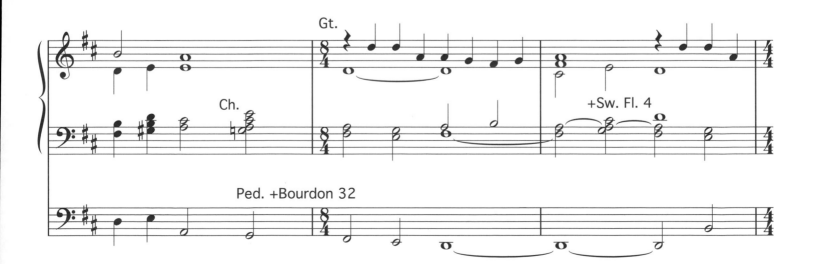

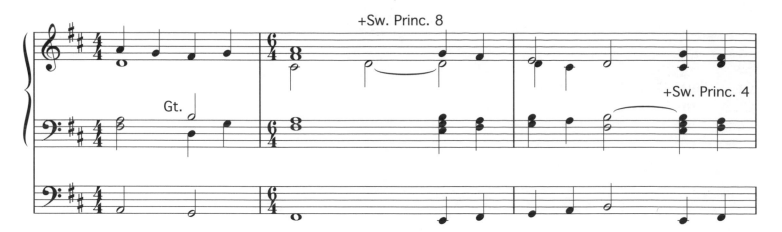

+Sw. Princ. 8

+Sw. Princ. 4

Gt.

cresc. to end

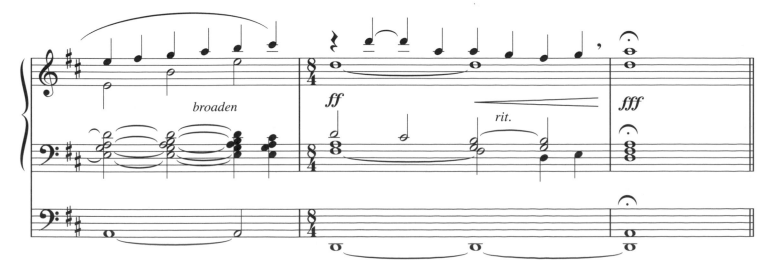

broaden

ff

rit.

fff

Allegro

Sw.   Foundations 8, 4, 2; Mixtures; Reeds 16, 8, 4; Sw. to Ch. 8, 4
Gt.   Enchamade Tpt. 8
Ch.   Foundations 8, 4, 2; Mixtures; Reeds 16, 8, 4
Ped.   Foundations 16, 8, 4; Sw. to Ped; Ch. to Ped.

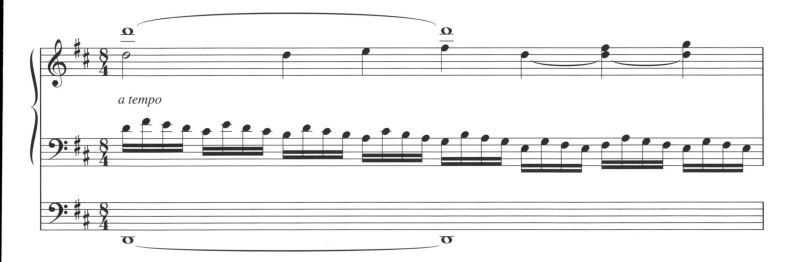

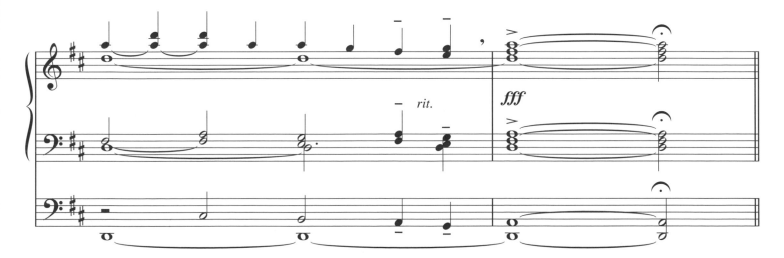

Sicilienne

Sw.   Flutes 8, 2
Gt.   8, 4, 2
Ch.   Flute 8; Sw. to Ch.
Ped.   Soft 16, 8; Sw. to Ped.

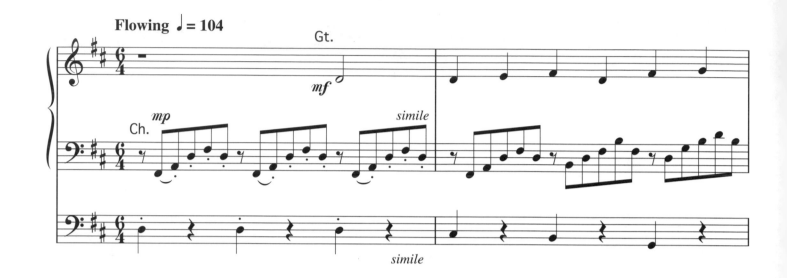

Adagio–Legato

Sw. Erzahlers; Sw. to Ch.
Gt. ----------------
Ch. Flute Celeste
Ped. Flute 4; trem.

Toccata

Sw.   Foundations 8, 4, 2; Mixtures; Sw. to Ch. 8; Sw. to Gt.
Gt.   Foundations 8, 4, 2; Mixtures
Ch.   Foundations 8, 4, 2; Ch. to Gt.
Ped. Clairon 4

Allegro ♩ = 112

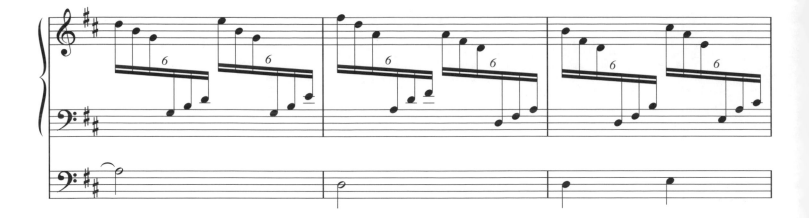

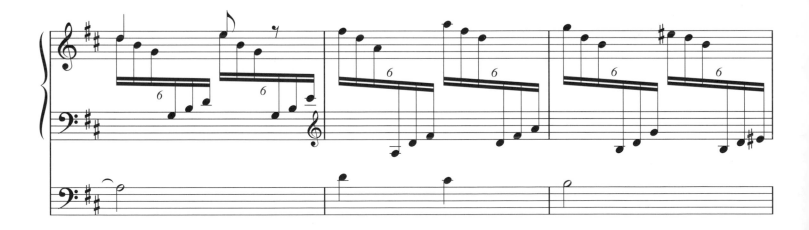

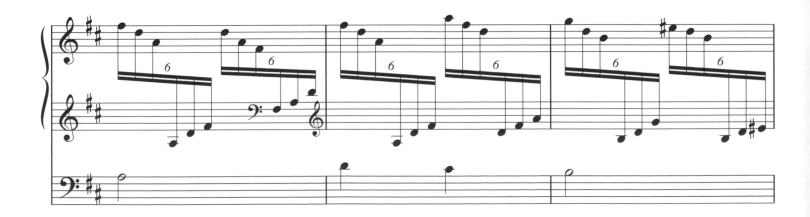

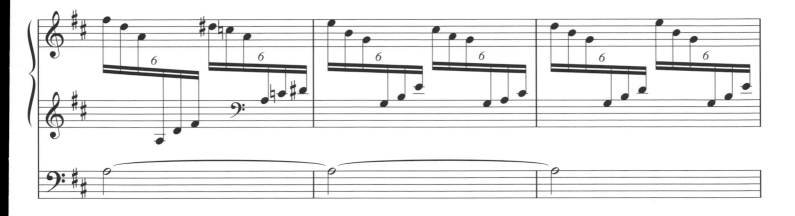

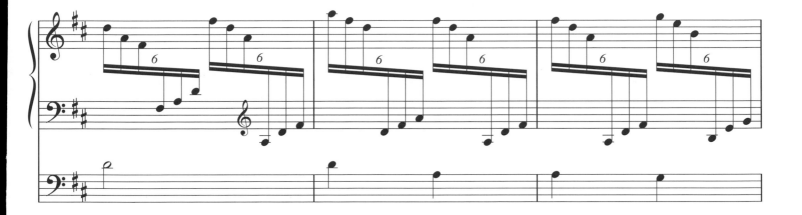

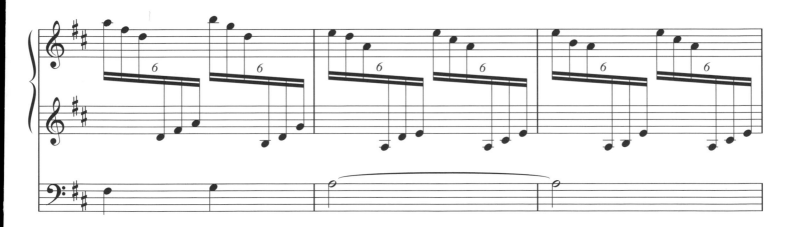

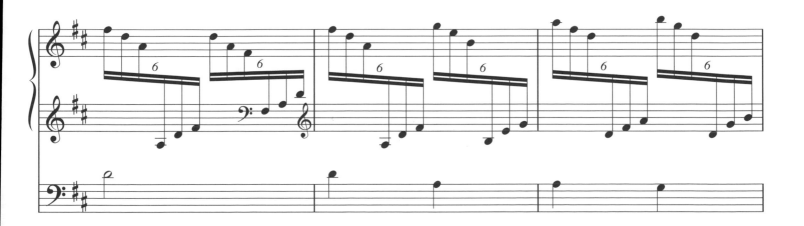

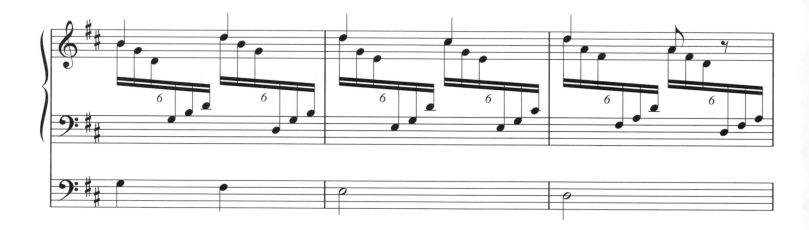

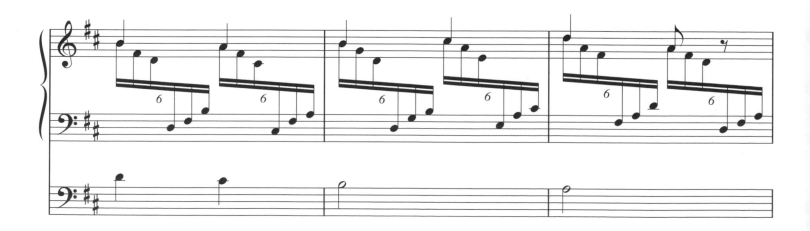

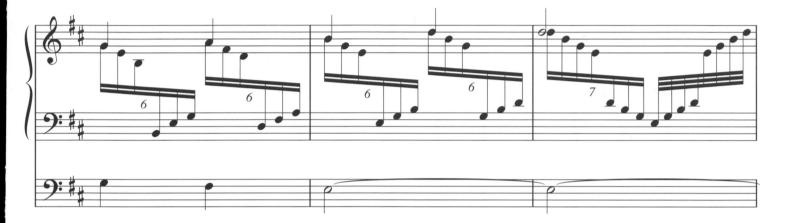

Ped. -Clairon 4
+Foundations 16, 8; Sw/Ch. to Ped.

+Sw. Reeds 16, 8, 4 (boxes closed)

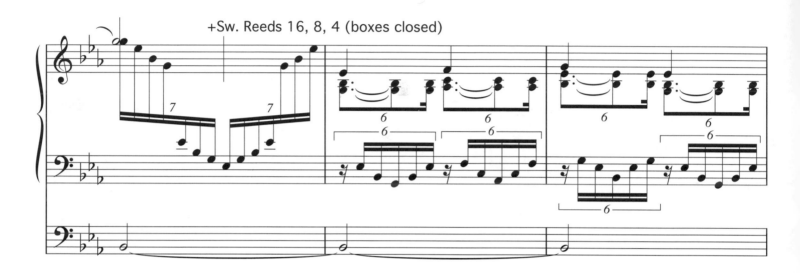

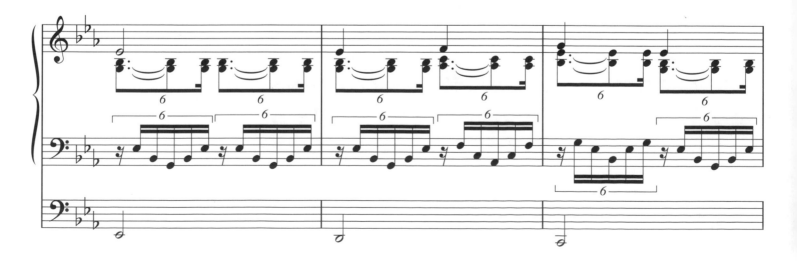

+Ch. Reeds 16, 8, 4   +Gt. Reeds 16, 8, 4

+Ped. Bombarde 16

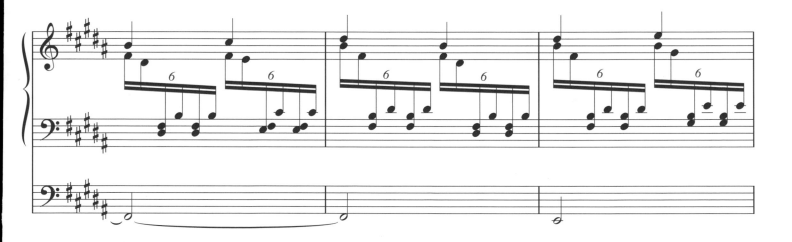

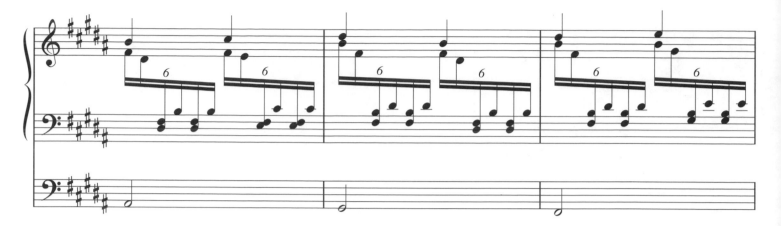

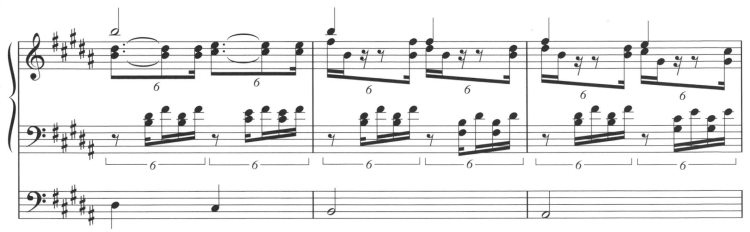

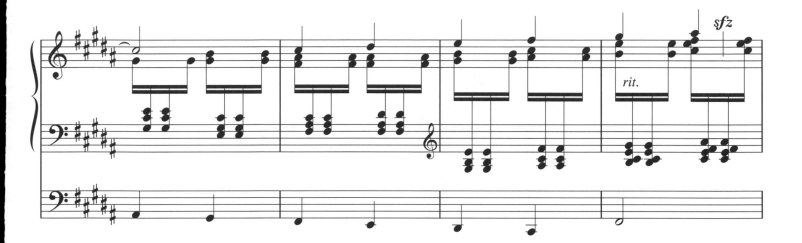

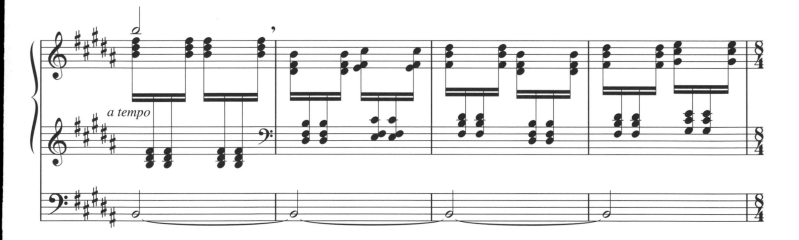

Please visit our website:
www.FredBock.com

EXCLUSIVELY DISTRIBUTED BY

HAL•LEONARD
CORPORATION
7777 W. BLUEMOUND RD. P.O. BOX 13819 MILWAUKEE, WI 53213

ISBN-13: 978-1-4234-0982-3

Distributed By
HAL LEONARD

08739896   9 781423 409823

8739896 All Creatures of Our God and King ORGAN BGK1036 $14.95

8 84088 05918 7